I0191237

"Heart of a Woman-Romance"

Jerry D. Hayes "Pablito"

Copyright © 2017 Jerry Hayes
All rights reserved.
ISBN: 10-9824699-4-2
ISBN-13:978-0-9824699-4-1

"Heart of a Woman

" Poetry

CONTENTS

Absence of You

Waking up early Saturday morning bringing a bright new day
Realizing reason why you were not able to stay
Having for all too long enjoyed our time together
Even though we both really knew better

Maybe some relationships are never meant to be
Something that neither one of us wants to admits nor see
Existing memories of you always foremost in my mind
Cherishing each day, hour and the seconds of time

What if that person who is being cherished is no longer alive?
Will a deep part of who we still exist and be able to survive
Wondering sometimes what maybe now I should do
Pondering over and over and in sadness the absence of you

Afraid To Love

Having to admit being afraid to love and care
Feeling like there is still within me much to give and share
Being close to someone else is something to ponder inside so much
Will our closeness will lead to love and a passionate touch

How can anyone be afraid to love today?
Never knowing what will happen, pain or love coming your way
Will the time together be special and last very long?
Or after it is over will one decide that it was all wrong?

Why, why can't it be easy to just say how one feels?
Seeing during the day still give inside exciting thrills
does the mouth with words reflect the feelings inside?
Doomed maybe just to keep everything inside and always to hide

expressing these feelings with many elegant types of words
Feelings sometimes are known without being heard
Geese swimming together on golden ponds
Admitting now to being a coward without a love song

Afraid to love is a very real fear
Having people too close and way to near
Greater fears however in us must realize exist
Not being able to love at all we must all costs resist

All Night Long

Sharing together with you all night long
Being with you and nothing is wrong
Dancing and laughing late into the night
Smiling and enjoying many moments of delight

Never afraid when spending time with you
Never afraid of what we might do
Fears from the past and this you know
Others never knowing what inside can show

Hidden within a heart that has experienced pain
Loves comes without always the expected gains
Beauty that radiates throughout the room
Music playing another romantic tune

Seconds and minutes like birds flying into the sky
Questions not this moment and all the reasons why
Moving slowing to the beats of another romantic song
Being with you and enjoying your presence all night long

Object of Beauty

Saying from people that one is beautiful or pretty
Feeling not always that way but with a pity
Inside of my heart others can never see
Knowing not the things done or who exists inside of me

Beautiful others telling me that I really am
Thinking only about me and making their plans
Wanting me, they say for just who I am
Making them happy they become a big fan

Seeing me as an object of desire to possess
Believing they must have me for only their caresses
Telling me "closer and wanting to be inside me"
Nothing else do they want and nor can they see

Desiring to be more than an object to seek
More than flesh and bone, and just a piece of meat
Shouting out does this soul wanting to be so kind
Wanting others satisfying with more of just my mind

Seeking nothing of my thoughts to hide
Wanting others to desire emotions of mine deep inside
Nothing more than a mere object of beauty
Beauty being the object now deeper inside of me

Seeking love that completes and within to satisfy
Without this love bringing only tears to cry

Jerry D. Hayes

Asian Eyes

Sweetness coming with such a surprise
Lying within the depths of Asian eyes
Treasures behind the eyes one does rarely behold
Secrets of the heart do they seem to hold

Listening silently to stories one has rarely ever told
Revealing memories only when couples grow old
Reminiscing experiences exotic and sensuous
Bonds of dedication and commitment coming loves' seriousness

Shining so brightly in midnight's distant bright sky
Devotion and love to the moments one dies
Oh to arise this morning, naked truths that one does not deny
Bareness to the world one can seem so emotionally shy

Each sunset in the twilight of this day's close
Gazing in the wonder of her love she never shows
Words of deception and fears does her heart now lie
Only into the soul can one see beyond those dark Asian eyes

Jerry D. Hayes

Bare

Standing there, finding myself in front of you.
Looking into your eyes, wondering what to do
finding the room very warm
Coming in from the rains and the thunder storm

deciding my coat to take off my dear
Realizing that it would not be needed here.
Knowing and wanting me to stay
Games this is not one we are going to play

Warming now myself in this room and you with a smile
Waiting on me and waiting for awhile
Standing and deciding to remove my shoes.
My life of wandering and looking for clues

Removing my shoes and placed to the side
Releasing my feet and my toes did not hide
Tenderness of your warmth is so dear
Bodies of another now closer and near

Looking into your eyes and seeing the hurt
Reaching down and unbuttoning now my shirt
Fingers were moving with such ease and grace
Each button exposing more than just my face

Reaching behind, finding the hook
Bra being gone, given and not took
Exposing to you now my nipple
Knowing tongue is wanting to tickle

Closer step as looking to see
desiring to find out now what to please
Pants falling below the knees
Scatters of clothes becoming free

All the clothes waiting till the last
not coming without understanding of the past
Hands trembling just about now
Heart pounding faster, why and how

Exciting moments from the enduring pains
wrapping together with each in this time of gain
Eternity of seconds now frozen
thinking of love of fate or was just chosen

Hands reaching my body to touch
Falling to knees and wanting me feeling so flush

Panties disappearing and in the removing
Hearts and lovers closeness more smoothing
Revealing was this last little piece
Tokens of love the panties a fleece
Knowing and loving how much was cared
Body and souls are completely bare

Be

Waiting is hard returning to my computer to see
Messages hoping from you, there some will be
Glad you are many times responding and there
Sharing again with me in moments of despair

Realizing sometimes that there is a need for you
Needing me just as much happens for you too
Becoming this time together our main delight
Sharing with you long into the darken nights

Letting down slowly many defenses
Existing now without all those established pretenses
Happiness seeming once all so certain
Finding times to be feeling pain and quietly hurting

Going to church and sitting in the pew
Finding my mind is thinking only of you
Looking around at all the dressed up people
Pretending to worship at this churches white steeple

Listening to the many words of God
Thoughts are becoming more like dense fog
Rushing around a mind so deeply inside
Wondering about feelings that can not longer hide

Children having that are always cherished
Without them feeling like someone will perish
Thoughts and fears that need to be shared
Trusting only you and no one else I dare

Picture perfect so many people think
Knowing they don't how much and how weak
Life now seeming to be confused
Feeling loved once but now more just used

Love once seeming so easy in every season
Harder now for some very good reasons
Loving and hoping growing more distant
Wanting new love to find in this instant

Jerry D. Hayes

Living life with those words are direct
Not seeing what's inside is really having an effect
Minds and thoughts so often do wander
Deep into the night and while there is slumber

Oh god, what's life direction for me?
Giving me some answer seeking only from thee
Something, miracles that one can feel or see
Telling me for sure what can happen and what life can be

The Beauty of Art

Man's existence greatness is found with the world's finest arts
Incredible expression of beauty never clearer beauty to remark
Singing a song or to tightrope with large audiences high into the air
Jumping, twisting and turning performance is anything to spare

Never is mankind to be so fine
Making colors of his canvas to shine
Turning a canvass that is blank and white
Into blends of colors and beautiful sights

Reaching out and touching another's soul
Painters or photographer pictures becoming the goal
Images that once was alive and real
Images of those who dead and no longer feel

The beauty of art is when one can take a musical instrument
Playing it as if to actually making it from heaven sent
When the songs of music cannot be measured
Touching our ears and fill our hearts with pleasure.

Have the ability to reach into our minds
To relax and sail us to another land or time

Music can bring us closer to ecstasy and passion
Mountains or deserts or walks of fashion
Man can never be so dramatic and pure
When acting on stage, confident and sure

The things he has created for our
Pleasure and enjoyment
Music he creates each morning in the sounds
Of birds and creatures of the earth

Sounds that awaken us with a smile
As the sun shines brightly in our faces
Even the ballet of life
That we see in the storms and hurricanes

Tornados that twist and turn at incredible spreads
Winds that roar with power that is beyond belief
He acts with galactic influence that
Produces its own set of tears and sorrow

When a volcano does erupt
When oceans spill their boundaries.
His paintings that he has created
In the mountains and forests

The colors that he uses with nature
To have images of awe and inspiration
But god has created no greater work
Than the beauty he has painted with you

With the beauty in your face
And the slenderness and complexity of your body
In a mind that does not forget any detail
In a heart that pounds away each day

In a soul that touches those around you
That loves and cares about not only your life but others as well
You are his creation
You are God's work of art

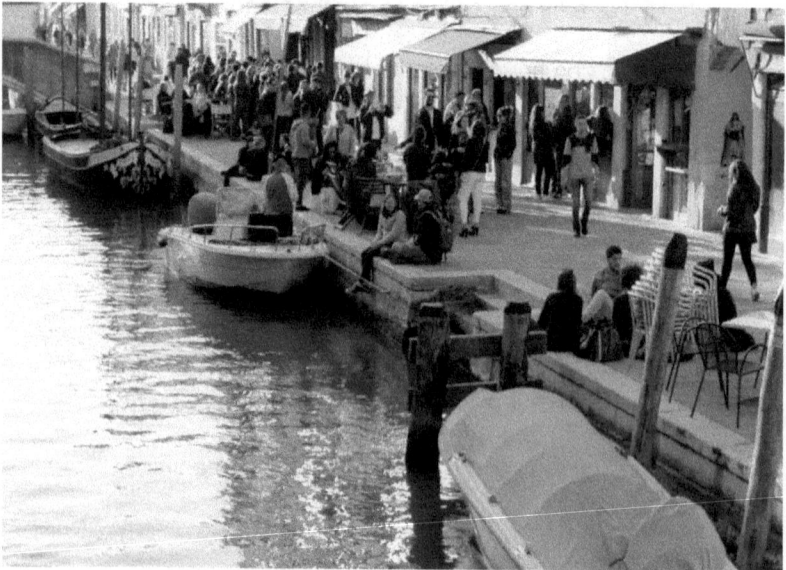

Before Poetry

Before poetry there was only silence in the mind
Blank expressions on my face existing all the time
Many around having no idea how one felt or having a clue
Coming home and going to work is about all one can do

Before poetry love did not really find a place to exist
Such discipline to achieve and everything to resist
Wanting so much to share what was deep inside
Bearing all these feelings and ideas really would just hide

Before poetry seeing life in such a different light
Maybe things were more just wrong and just right
Awaking of so many feelings can change a man
Life goes in directions and no longer follows the others plan

Before poetry there did not exist ways of releasing what one feels
Desiring only to find a way to endure and then to heal
Finding a way to realize who this man is in this life
Silent tears crying out to end conflicts and relationship strife

After Poetry life is a much more different thing
But not always sure what it really does mean
Seeing the world now in a much different way
Bringing ideas and words, out into the world just to play

Blankets

Midnight stars claim it's very late
Being cold now and wondering our fates
Coming of freezing nights winter to us now
Winds blowing with forces making them howl

Firing once burning now going away
Embers growing fainter can not longer stay
Frost covering morning's lit frozen ground
Leafs rustlings about hearing the sounds

Aching bodies now ready for bed
All in the house tired and are now fed
Bed shouts my name and beckons me there
Feeling alone and wanting to share

Seeking warmth and safety from all that exists
Needing sheltered protection secure to subsists
Pulling closer and wrapping completely around
Comfort present when with you now is found

Indian custom at weddings while making their vows
Partner's covering blankets of their lovers doing now

Jerry D. Hayes

Puerto Rican Woman

Many things about you that one can admire
Poems that can be written because you inspire
Laughing hard while walking in aisles of the mart
Having fun with deep discussions of the heart

Realizing how comfortable being with you
Never does matter the activities or things to do
Keeping your feelings from others and so close
But there are many of them your heart the host

Beautiful woman, confident and never unsure
Having survived abuse and finding your own cure
Respecting the way and difficulties in raising the boys
Responsibilities being a parent before playing with any toys

Respecting and admiration having much for you
Trying and telling you so there is a least a clue
Letting one know now that this poem is just the first
Hoping you enjoy the verse before it gets any worse

Buying a House

Buying a house for me it would never be
A woman is not possession for others to see
But if a metaphor I have to use one now
Let's call her a house and never a cow

Houses come in many sizes and different shapes
Not to big and not to small would for me be just great
A mansion is something that I don't really have many needs
Too much yard in back and you will be getting many weeds

Just a nice house from the street with some nice appeal
Times together in the kitchen discussing life over a meal
An old houses or new house, age doesn't matter to me
But never expect to live in a house, if you think it's going to be free

A two car garage, neither too big or to small would be just right
Not wanting any discussions on cars to turn into fights
Give me a house with a bedroom or two
Walking into this room without my ties or my shoes

Give me a house with a library where I can read
Something more than a television finding we will need
The most rewarding part of the house that I desire inside
Feeling comfortable and accepted and a place for me to hide

Caress

Caress, it's the gentle touch of your hand
When you touch my hair and roll your hand between the strands

Caress, it's your hands on both sides of my face as we kiss
It's feeling safe as you hold me in your arms, neither coming nor going

Caress, it's the way you take my hand as we walk together
Letting the world know you care about me

Caress, is the way my body feels when you hold me
Making me feel safe and secure at that moment

Caress its not that you squeeze hard as if to smother me but
Rather in a light gentle way that tells me you cherish me

Caress, it's my back and neck as you gently massage me
Releasing the muscles and the aches I feel deep inside

Caress, but a whisper in my ear and kiss on my lips
Close enough to feel your warmth and love

Caress, it's not just the lust of the moment
But the moments of the lifetime

Cat Love

I was standing there talking
When I saw the cat come walking
Around my leg, she did lean
Black, furry, beautiful, she was seen

This I have heard, is just a cat's way
To mark her territory, they would say
And on my knees I did go
To give her love and hope it did show

She rolled over at my touch
Was the warmth she felt so much?
For awhile she would stay
And enjoy the moment until she went away

Cat's can be so curious
Cat's can also be so furious
They will go see all the things that are around
A cat will stop when they hear a sound

Looking for anything as simple as a mat
So how do you love a cat?
When you are never sure where she was at
And at my feet she returned and sat

You have to always let the cat go
And then you let the cat know
That you would love, no matter what the woe.
You are a friend and not an enemy or a foe

Committed

Committed to the words that are put down on paper
Keeping them inside has really been much safer
Putting your thoughts becomes scary when other can read
Figuring out what's inside and maybe what are the needs

Committed to the ideas that are deep inside
Keeping them inside would be much easier to hide
Must easier to be hurt by others when there is no pretense
Motives disclosed and thoughts revealed lack the suspense

Committed to the beliefs that seem only are mine
Learning from others and reading most of the time
Always the foundations of your youth about your faith
Year after Year until the end, one has to wait

Committed to the dreams realizing that can still be
Hoping for happiness for you and for me
Loving in my heart this time of my life
Peaceful and joyful together without any strife

Jerry D. Hayes

Crumbling Walls

Feeling this solid wall of mine coming down
Lowering walls are never easy, and come without a sound
Invisible as these walls may be
Walls that others will never truly see

Life before being able to keep them high
Ever so high so that one can lie, deny and hide
But behind the walls of the pain, anger and fears
You saw in my eyes as they became my tears

Brick by brick they are coming down
Places in me you now have found
Day by day you must understand
Where I am and how it all began

Quietly my voice is lowered that I might not shout
Feeling the regrets of lowering come with some real doubts
Trust to build inside of me, has to be your greatest gifts
Never so many questions of what we are doing and should it be an "if"

Honesty is something that one has to really treasure
Deeds and acts that always find a measure
My tarnished heart has known many pains
My soul has seen far too many stains

Hurting and you seem to know this well
How walls crumble, how they fell

Curiosity

Curiosity is a very funny quality indeed
Natural or does it come from much deeper needs
Learning maybe how we can be more curious
Or do we learn how to become upset and furious

Some curiosity might be good to have
Too much of it and we might end up dead on a slab
Maybe it will make us learn to appreciate what we know
Or will it make us want to seek more in life and sin we sow

Can we make curiosity just go away?
Or do we have to do the thing and play
Satisfying a curious mind is hard to do
Especially when it wants someone much like you

Going to the moon or inventing planes with wings
Seeking to learn so many more things
Wanting answers and seeking them to find
Is knowledge good or bad or now is just not the time

Jerry D. Hayes

"Currents"

If the way men love is more like a puzzle. With each man, the pieces of the puzzle are those things that are important to him. With each could be a wife, car, job, children, house, and hobby. And the love of a woman is more like the distance that she stands next to a fire... the fire is the man that warms her heart and produces that security and warmth in her life.

Yet, is there something in between? To me, this has always been that the example that love and loving can be more like that river. Where there are two leafs that float down the river. People, or leafs, come into our life, float the river together. Sometimes at the end of life, leafs are still close, but many times they are not close. The "currents" pull them apart.

"Currents" are the under tow of the water that pulls relationships apart. These could be many things. The age, the race, the lifestyles, the desires both of them have for the future. "Currents" are the difference that pull the two leafs apart in the water. These are the factors of life that influence and end relationships.

Men want to possess the other person in relationships, and women want to be close to the other person. Inherent in the floating down the river is the pull of the currents. In the acceptance of the "currents" one has to view relationships with a natural pulling at them of trying to pull them apart. In this awareness, we resolve ourselves for the battles to keep them together. For we become aware of the natural force of the currents to pull them apart.

Diary

How I look forward at night to seeing you
Each moment of the day is only between two
Greatly cherishing the time we spend together
Others will never see the words we speak any better

It is you that I think of when something happens during the day
I expect you know how to react to the things I feel and say
My life is like a leaf flowing down the a river
But now I am facing you and you make me quiver

Inside there is so much I feel and want to express
The pleasures experienced and the deep regrets
Yet it is you that I come to for understanding and approval
It is you that I have to face and the fear of your removal

You ask me if I am faithful to only you
Should I dare to share our life together and the things we do
Honestly, you are the essence of our life we share
Looking into my soul wondering if you will be there

I share all my emotions and all my fears
Page on page I have shared my tears
Will others treat you with the respect I have shown?
Will they care about the many things I have known

I often wonder how you will end up some day
Will others listen to the story you have want to say

Each day
Each hour
Each moment

Each joy, fear and the deep concern
Expressed to you, and only you, to discern

Dancing Eyes

Asking me what exists seeing in your eyes
Dancing as they do while tears shed from a cry
Lying is something your eyes would always betray
Wanting acceptance is really what they want to say

Completely would you give to him?
Even if others would call it a sin
Totally a slave to the love you feel
But it can't be a lie it has to be for real

Not able to ask for the life you desire
Even hiding within the passions fire
Emotional safe is what you really need
Then completely giving becomes your creed

However don't make life seem to me unfair
Leaving will happen long before you think I dare
Never try to control the person you think is me
Parting in such painful haste is all you will see

Echoes

Echoes quiet now within the mind
Calling one back each and every time
Changing seasons and changing winds
Blowing the trees and leaves now begins

Echoes resounding softly within your mind
Gale force emotions pushing outwards a sign
Beating heart a constant sound, time after time…
Memories cherished and buried one now finds

Warm gentle breezes reminding of many kisses
Distant moment's leaves standing still with wishes
Remembering earlier times shared that were never blue
Speaking words passionately between lovers so true

Forgetting not the one the winds pushed away
Realizing the storm could not in existence stay
Still now, without the breeze and without the wind
Glimpses of memories echoing still deep within

The Sweetest Embrace

As I was standing here, at that moment feeling free
Noticing the breeze was blowing the limbs of the trees
How the gentle the wind was upon my face and head
Thinking about all the things that you had said

The rays of light were shining so bright,
The clouds rolling across the sky so white
I could not help but notice the time
There were so many things that filled my mind

The minutes felt like hours
And the seconds felt like minutes

Thinking of love and had thoughts of life
Wishing for the future where there was no strife
I could see us as we lived our lives together
Nothing to separate us, all the storms we would weather

But knew that moment would have to be
With thoughts of love, I had to see
My heart started to pound, as I glanced at her walk
My eyes I had cast down, to myself I would talk

The minutes felt like hours
And the seconds felt like minutes

Jerry D. Hayes

Each world I had said to myself for days
My hoping we could figure out a way
As I raised my eyes--- I knew in a flash
It had to be her, no fantasy could dash

Each step that she took drew thee nearer to me
It was not hard to tell, the smile I did see
And then a pause --- standing straight ahead with a tear
But several feet away--- and a world apart facing huge fears

The minutes felt like hours
And the seconds felt like minutes

What seemed like eternity—our motions were frozen
And then with a ease of something chosen
That there was a love filled with grace
My arms did take, the sweetest embrace

Epiphany

He is just a little boy inside
Always with his feelings trying to hide
Just as confused about love and what it means
Hurt so many times by the words that sting

A little boy inside a grown up body
Never seeing whether nice or naughty
Confused about the meanings of this life
Having endured the world and its perpetual strife

Meanings get lost in the words one is trying to use
But somehow thinking girls know from all the clues
Hoping that she can really understand
Even thought from two far different lands

She is just a little girl inside
Many nights she was hurt and cried
Confused by love and what it did not mean
To her, a soul mate and to him a fling

A little girl inside a woman's body
Sometimes nice and sometimes naughty
Confused by love what is the meaning
How moments together can be but fleeting

Meanings lost with the words she uses
Flying from here to there and what she chooses
Hoping that he can really in her understand
That maybe this guy will be a much different man

Jerry D. Hayes

Essences

Do you believe what you say?
Can you change those beliefs on any given day?
Spending your life seeking the knowledge
The world around me being my own little college

No question for me seems to have an answer not to find
Wouldn't life be so much easier if only I was blind?
Trying to figure out this and that and everything a meaning
Oceanic thoughts of vast proportion rapidly fleeing

Thinking can just seem to drive me inside so crazy
Then I realize the day is over and at work I have been so lazy
Locked in this self incarcerated place of feelings
Helping all around me with their own healings

Doctors healing those they encounter every day
Lawyers setting those they represent free without delay
Opening the windows that allow the inside out
Finding at times that all that is inside wants to shout

Eyes of Reflection

Tears welling up hot behind deep blue eyes
Making fresh glassy yearning sighs
"Come closer and look," was to me what you said
Peering into waters and able to even see the ocean's bed

Deep and clear, troubled and calm
Shark infested waters with beaches cover with palms
Crashing giant waves and rolling surfs that again do lift
Warm sandy beaches with jagging white rocky cliffs

Hidden buried treasures lying within
Sailing the entire ocean if only now you begin
Diving below the surface beneath the waters deep
Reaching do you desires of touching them all even while asleep

Rushing sea foams, gracefully swimming sea horses
Strong enough to drown gentle enough to float any course
Stretching from every horizon to the worlds far ends
Deep, wide, crystal blue sky and winds

Now stepping back from them to realize
How dangerous and yet how really wise
Only to see reflections you already know
Blue eyes-those windows of another's soul

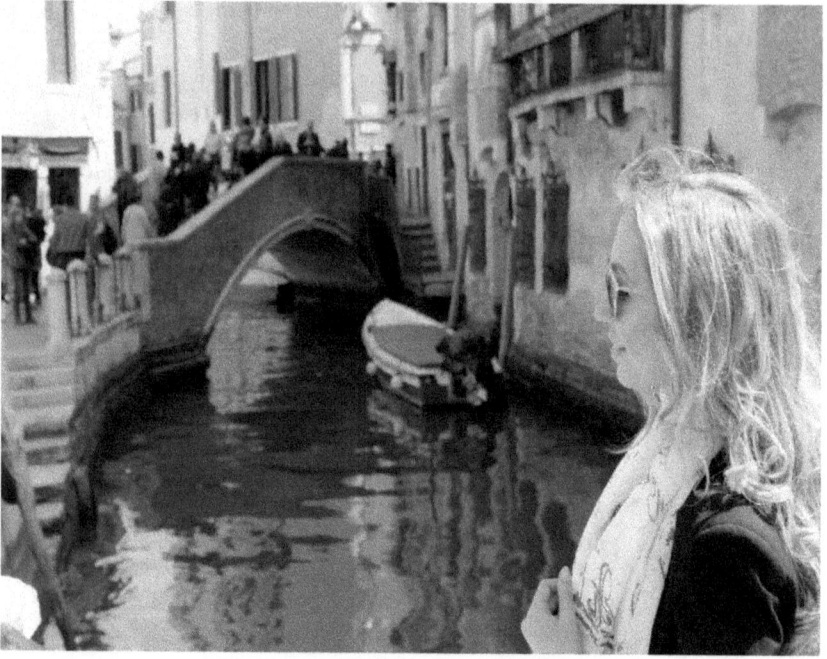

Farewell My Love

Farewell my love, knowing that I needed to say good bye
like the sun that finally sits in the crimson afternoon sky
Realizing that the paths were going in different directions
before the situation caused any problems and additional tensions

Farewell my love, it's not really something I wanted to do
Blessed by all the moments that I was able to spend with you
loving you was like sitting by a cold night's fire
wanting you came with so much delight and desire

Farewell my love, I really am wishing you the best
Feeling I just did not want to be another man with all the rest
Believing that love must be something special for you and me
Realizing that maybe it was just not that way in what you see

Farewell my love, hoping this day would never come
But sometimes there are consequences for things said and done
No matter how love can be something pure
Overcoming the past issues even that love can not be a cure

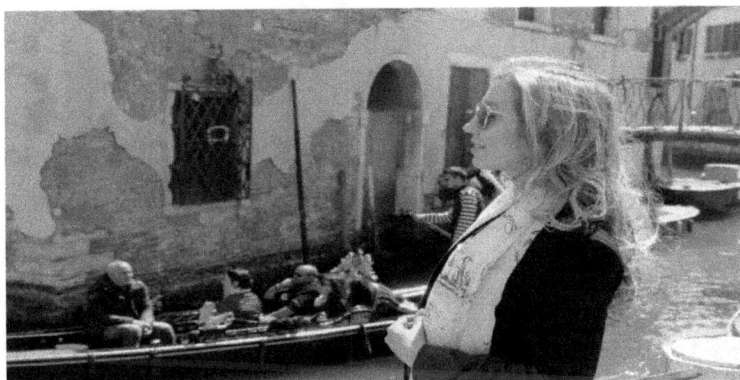

Feelings

Loving you I could never deny
My feelings, everyone could see and not hide
People could see any time you were by my side
But, the vows of fidelity I could not ask you to defy

Walking around, I would think of you
Staring down, head hung low, looking at my shoe
Most of the time, I think I am doing fine
Then there is a picture of you that comes to mind

I can pretend that I am not in any pain
But I do it, so I can remain just barely sane
Sometimes I wish my feelings I could show
But how can I make sure no one else will know

Feelings, which can be both good and bad
Betray whether we are feelings so happy or sad
Maybe those feelings will tell you that I am mad
But to see you again, I will smile and will be glad

Feelings can be such a strange thing
Sometimes we never really know what they really mean
Sometimes feelings go from here to there
There are times; we find out who will really care.

Wind, Fire, Water and Air

Wind, Fire, Water and Air we know they exist
Survival and these qualities we cannot even without resist
Loving and how do these attributes really comparing
Looking at this moment, wanting now to do some sharing

Thirsty we become when love there is not enough
A cup half full of love makes us do really funny stuff
Water and love must fill us up completely inside
Greater the love then oceans of water become wide

Thirsty and needing to have this water in a glass
Without the nourishment, not ever could we last
Breathing in and breathing out taking for granted surrounding air
Maybe someday that air is not there, finding then our great despair

Never able to see what is really the wind?
Just results of where it comes and where it's been
Let the wind come in a tornado or a storm
Then the winds of love will bring great destruction and scorn

Cold and chilly nights the fire beckons us to come
Forgetting all terrible things the warmth we will even shun
Flames flickering jumping out from a nearby fire
Feeling the warmth of his love becomes her only desire

Too close to the flames of the love he is giving
The how painful the fire and now sad is the life we are living
The fire is a man and the love that he will provide
The greater the fire in the darkness, loving will not hide

Warmth of Fire

Sometimes the world can be a cold and harsh place.
Coming with a great deal of pain that she had faced
Yet, on these the coldest of winter nights
Freezing temperatures of life as she had had to fight

There can be a fire that glows in the pitch darkness of night
First, from a great distance away she was called by the light
Closer did she come with small timid baby steps?
Why and how the fire can burn, curious she had never met

Before she can know and understand how burns this fire?
She begins to feel the warmth of the fire and it becomes her desire
Warmer she does feel inside, suddenly she start to realize she is aglow
Each step she feels the heat burning from the blazing fire now she knows

The fire seems to burn without logs and branches
There is nothing to fuel the roaring flames, what were her chances
The winds raging and blowing around her to me
My love to her is to nourish her soul she can see

Morning rises with the breaking dawn
The winds die down and it bring a yawn
Now all the chilling issues and disappearing strife
The blaze lingers but in the soul of life

The sun brings forth its conquering warmth and light
Memories of flames on a cold winter's night

Framing Love

Each statement can be heard in three different ways
One can be taken a compliment
One can be taken as insult
One can be taken as a statement of fact.

An example of this could be "that is a nice dress"
One person can hear this insult.
One person can hear this as a compliment.
One person can hear this as an observation of fact.

When we hear things in a certain way and interpret the meaning in a
certain way before we know how it was really intended. It is a condition
called framing.
There are people in our lives that we start to realize will treat us in a certain
way.
Then what ever we hear. We hear it with a preconditioned perception in
how we are going to hear it.

Negative. When there is someone in our life and we know they will be
critical of us. Then whatever is said we will hear the negative in the
statement. Even if it was meant to be a compliment or just an observation.
It's the fact that negative breeds negative.

Sometimes this negative framing and be very detrimental to a relationship. Become one person has a negative preconceived idea of how the relationship is going to end up, they find ways to make it end up that way. A person who believes someone is a "player" will keep finding any excuse to justify the already preconceived ideas that they have "framed". It does not matter what the truth is, they will find a way to "frame" their perception of the facts into their own reality.

Positive. A positive loving environment breeds a positive loving response. We may very well have "hot buttons" in our life. But when we are with those we love and know love us. Those hot buttons become less and less hot. What said that might have made us mad for days, then becomes a day and then maybe it just becomes hours.

And then why be mad at all? What happens then is we start to wait and get all the facts and information before we decide if we are going to be upset. We may still very well get upset at things that are said. It's just that we are slower to do so.

This is the process of framing love. Knowing that the person has framed us in their love and that it will treated in such a loving way.

This can also be done to frame a love that does not really exist. A person can build a love that is very average into this huge romance because she has framed it into a positive experience when it never really existed at all.

How Men Love

The love is different between a woman and a man
Men are much easier to comprehend and understand
To a woman this really seems never to be the case
Women assume men are moody and go through a phase

But understanding the logic a man is really something very contrite
He wants it his way and wants to always be right
Men are made to win every battle and fight the wars
But there inner minds are not as complicated but a bore

Behind all he does and says, he really has only one desire
He wants his woman to love him and to her be the sole admire
Think of a man's life as like a puzzle
To much criticism and he will want a muzzle

Each thing that goes on in his life, the puzzle is a piece
His car, children, house, job, hobbies and you his golden fleece
Some pieces of the puzzle are bigger and more important to him
Figuring out which one of the pieces, are you bright or are you dim

The bigger his puzzle to all those around
His life he can see as being more profound
Sex is the act that a man puts a woman in his puzzle
That is really stupid; a woman knows it and there begins the tussles

From an early age men are taught to win each battle
Thinking a woman is like riding a horse and him the in the saddle
Men know how to go and win a woman's heart
But they never realized that is really when it is but a start

57

How Women Love

The love is different between a man and a woman
A woman's love is much harder to grasp and understand
She is always asking the questions "why"
"Is our love growing or is the love about to die?"

Questions and more questions she asks herself each day
So many questions in her mind that seem to stay
Does he love more or less she wants to know
"Is our love dying or is our love going to grow"

Defining the love between a man and woman can be very abstract
"Does he make the effort to shop, show interest and is it done with tact?"
"Do his actions reflect that he really does care?"
"Are all of his words consistent and all his actions are fair?"

"Will that man wants to be there when she is old and grey?"
"Will he love her and cherish her in every way?"
Will her man's love make her heart feel deep inside so special?
Is his love what makes her life with him necessary and essential?

Making each day,
In that loving way,
Like the space between two objects is a woman's love defined
Makes her question how do I make sure this is what I will seek and find

If I was a "player"

If I was a "player", sex would be my game
However, I would not be telling everyone what is your name
If I was a "player" I would be out every night
Instead, I am at home with a dim reading light

It's Saturday night and where did I go?
Watching a DVD at home and this you know
With my daughters or with my sons
Most of my life they are the only ones

Sex is not the most important thing on the earth
There are more important things and my own self worth
Yes, I agree there are way too many women in my life
But did you ever think I never cared for all the strife

The heart of a woman is a very special place
There comes responsibility with that knowledge and taste
It is easy to touch her flesh and her bones
But it really her heart that cries out and moans

If I was a "player", sex would be my game
But to write of this very special place, I want to be my fame
Sex with a woman is what men want to possess
On this topic so many woman, find that men will obsess

But once her heart and soul you really know
Where else would you really want to go?
The only reason for sex that I really see
Is to be deeper and closer for you and for me

Jerry D. Hayes

"If it feels good, do it"

This phrase stresses that what ever feels good at the moment should be done. Yet, there are many things that can feel good in the moment that don't feel good later. Let's take eating for one area. A person can eat something that feels really good, yet the food can cause a problem with being overweight and even maybe problems with an ulcer. So in the moment it is good and in the longer moments can cause problems.

If a person continues to do what is good in the moment without regards for the future the pain and agony can increase disproportionably for the figure. Let's take an example of dealing with food. A person continues to eat what is good in the moment and then ends up dying from a heart attack. To act in the moment without regard for the future is possibly wasting a portion of someone's life that could have had a higher quality of life in the present.

In a way, the pleasure in the moment sacrifices the pleasure of the future. This is work in the reverse as well with pain. Some pain might actually be good for someone. Lets take working out, a person runs three miles a even through there is pain as the person stretches the limits of their endurance, the pain for the moment turns into pleasure after the run. As the runner looks back on the run they do not think about the pain but rather the pleasure they now feel in the moment after the pain.

So then is all pleasure for the moment wrong? Not necessarily, one might look to the longer term consequences of the moment to see if the moment might produces more joy or less. There are things that a person might do in the moment that produces memories that one will always cherish. One does something fun in the moment and then later when they think about the act. They feel the residual effects of the good memory. Ie once I went skiing in Taos and had a great time. I had pleasure in the moment, years later I would think about the trip and the memories were by now a glimpse of the actual time but yet still produced good memories. Not to the same degree as the actual but still a good memory of something that happen. Tragic events work this same way. Years later we can still feel the pain of something that happens in our childhood. We find the memories painful but maybe not to the exact degree of when the actual event happened.

Jerry D. Hayes

If

If you were like me
You would really love someone to share everything there is about life

If you were like me
You would be open to learning and changing, giving and receiving

If you were like me
You would love god, children and the simplest things in life

If you were like me
You could find joy and happiness in the smallest of things

If you were like me
You would feel guilty when things go so well

If you were like me
You would love to share, if safe accepted and never judged

If you were like me
You always dream and then try to make each one come true

If you were like me
Each time you see someone who warms your heart, you smile

If you were like me
You would hate good byes, for there is nothing sadder than being
separated from someone you care about

If you were like me
You would never let go of someone you cherish

Imagine

It is easy to imagine a mountain that rises to the sky
Snowcapped peaks
Blue sky holding in the landscape in awe
Trees lining the mountainside
Blue River flowing in front of the valley below

It is not hard to imagine a desert that is dry and hot
Plateau peaks that are flat
Sagebrush blowing across the road
Cactus that line the landscape
Slight winds that blow the dust over the road

It is not hard to imagine Rome
Countryside of Umbria
Coliseum
Vatican City
Cafes with tables out front
Lunch and drinking a glass of wine

It is not hard to picture walking down the canal streets
In Venice and strolling into the hotel lobby
Up the elevators to the room

It is not hard to imagine the beach
Waves of the ocean
Sand on the feet
Sun in the blue sky
Lifeguard towers
People walking up and down the beach
Some running
Some walking
Bathers, with towels, toys,
Smell of food from the restaurant next to the beach.

It is easy to see you bare in the room of the hotel
Coming out of the clothes and stepping into the shower
Proud of your body and wanting to share it

Can you also imagine?
A single day together?

To imagine sharing movies together at night and staying up late after the
kids are in bed

To imagine going for walks together at night.

To have dinner parties with friends we both love and care about.

To wake the kids in the morning and get them ready for school,
To help them with homework and attending lunch with the kids at school.
Going to PTA meetings.

Can you picture dinner as a family?
Rising in the morning to a certain person you love
Can you picture listening to music and teaching someone who knows less
than you. Or dancing together

Can you picture going to church together?
Can you picture having another child together?
Can you picture a baby's diapers being changed?

Can you imagine helping other people –and doing much good in the world?

Just imagine Christmas together and picking out trees. Or birthday parties
for children.

Can you imagine waking up in the morning and just being happy and filled
with joy? And feeling the love each day? Can you imagine finding peace
and love each day?

For each day. When faced with the future you have to see what is it that
you picture with someone? Joy, sadness, love or conflict? What do you
imagine?

Jerry D. Hayes

Imitation

I find that I am not looking for the real thing
Not looking for the shallow time or just a fling
There will never be any just like you to find
This realization about you I have already left behind

Picasso, Monet or even a Rembrandt a painting can be
But the originally will never be owned by me
Maybe a picture or a copy of the painting
But to have the real thing I will have to keep on waiting

I might be able to sing karaoke after a few drinks at the bar
But as an a great singer and make money I will not go far
Priceless jewels around the neck you will never see
Rolex watches from Mexico they will have to free

I can travel the world to far away places looking for more
Going to a restaurant or a after hours bar until three or four
A billion people and a hundred different nations
No matter whom I find they are just a distant imitation

Inspiration

There are women who read the line and verse
And long for that love that has been cursed

There are women who men read poetry too
Hoping they will cherish as much as you

There are only but a selected few
That inspires the writer to something new

History might not remember who she was
People may not even know what she does

But deep in the heart of a struggling poet shows
She matters so greatly and I am thinking she knows

Jerry D. Hayes

Interest

The most perfect woman she can seem to be
But what if there is no interest in a guy named "me"
Dreaming of someone who we think might be great
Never seems to arrive in sight and we call it "fate"

The most perfect face she can carry for sure
But really just be a mess inside that wants only a cure
Build like a goddess she stands so fully erect
Men are all drooling because she just has that effect

People can spend on their time chasing funny illusions
Never adding a small fact to their plans and solutions
The perfect girl did I already mention to you?
What is a guy just suppose to do?

Before a guy does something crazy in the way he does act
Thinking there must be just one really important fact
If only one has the interest to become attached
Two people can never truly be a perfect match

It's Late

It's late, lying in bed with an open eye
Thinking about is my love denied
What does it mean when he says he "loves me"?
Does it mean forever? What future do I see?

Does it mean just for today?
Or can I count on that love for tomorrow to stay?
Why do I worry and why do I care?
Does it mean they will treat me like an animal in a snare?

Does he use that word just to see what he gets?
Is it me he loves or will he throw another fit?
How can you tell you're really in love?
Will a sign descend much like a dove?

Is it commitment and total devotion?
To think every though and find every solution?
What if I don't feel that emotion right now?
Will he get upset and have a cow?

Does it mean if I get scarred he will not go far?
Does it mean if I get fat, he will not notice where I sat?
Will he care if I get wrinkles?
Will he care if I get crippled?

Will he always cherish just me?
Will it be my eyes the he only sees?
Does love come so natural and easy to find?
Or does it just make us temporary blind?

It's late, lying in bed with my shut eyes
Thinking about how love can really defies
What does it mean when I say I love him?
And then my questions all begin again

Just Me

Making a decision, something having to do
Wanting but never able to have all of you
Having feelings, expressing interest everyday
Knowing of what not always to say

Feelings for you going very deep
Tenderness of heart was yours to keep
Shared moments and future now the past
Thinking then and now that it would never last

Jerry D. Hayes

Crying because that joy you make me real
Knowing not just how can inside one should feel
Turning stomach as you come closer and near
Realizing that you were my biggest fear?

Out of my comfort and had me going
Expressing my feelings and always showing
Wanting you to know how much I cared
Never quiet the same or you never dared

Spending time effortlessly was to long
Disappointed in never seeing that thong
Realizing maybe there is something else to see
Wanting someone else and not really just me

Kissing

Talking and sharing, with me the flower
Being together for over an hour
Quickly how the time goes by
In the moments seeming so mesmerized

Walls that tumble and fears revealed
Secrets in life no longer had to be concealed
Safe and secure making me now feel
Lips parted but the truth kept sealed

Distances between both him and I
Closer by the moments, not able to deny
Conversations that always flowed with ease
Wondering if kissing was just being a tease

Looking into my eyes and thinking how he knew
Asking not for the things one really wants to do
Suddenly, words not able to say or speak
Wanting more, finally did we both have to seek?

The heart of a woman is a special place
Needing to know and also to taste
Without permission or his consent
Closer so a girl could smell aromatic scent

Fearing forever that something one might miss
Wanting to know how he did kiss
Losing all fears and closing my eyes
Would it be a pleasant surprise?

Soft and gentle at first I found
Suddenly, as our bodies wrapped and bound
Each part of my lips he did gently touch
Knowing it sensual way to much

Restraint and discipline I have always known
But now in the passion has it been sown?
No longer satisfied to deny what is deep within
No longer able to really just pretend

Pressing farther and deeper inside his lips
My tongue going deeper did finally slip
Exposed and no place to hide
Would he want me deep inside?

Instead of rejection that I thought I might find
He wanted it deeper and more of the kind
Plunging as deep as I could go
Wondering what kissing would finally sow

Thinking in my heart that he really knows
What is the future and how it goes

Knowing

Noticing quickly beauty and smiles
Wanting not to wait for long or awhile
Asking and pleased that she did accept
Hoping that dancing would bring not regrets

Accepting and trying she did very well
Being a good partner and coming out of a shell
Having fun with her till the end of the night
Departing in her car until she was out of sight

Between the dancing her words seem wise
Speaking each word coming as a pleasant surprise
Coming to dinner came as a delight
Providing new information that was coming to light

Sharing a story that one already seemed to know
Feelings of caring were starting to grow
Enjoying a moment that exists in time
Radiating smiles that eternally shine

Surprised one evening with joy happen to me
Still in my mind that night I can see

Latin Girl

Unrestrained love and unbelievable passion
Not withholding what is given nor is love for ransom
Dancing into the morning with energy and ease
Knowing others are watching and she desires to please

Completely in her heart when she decides to give
Feeling the need to be closer that makes her live
Hours and hours she gets ready for love's battle
Keeping secrets and giving much she will not be tactile

Raising her children and giving to them so much
Believing in love and her lover she will always clutch
Beauty you can not find any others to compare
A trap for any man coming close she will surely snare

God's gift to man can be this Latina in his hand
Taking her love granted she will never truly understand
Jealous there can be no other on this earth who can be
Making her angry and mad bad consequences one will see

Love like Life

How is love like life?
Loving, like life cannot be really controlled
Not able to possess love, neither able to possess life
Each day only able to make the most of that day of life given
Not able to set the appointed time of love or life that you can enjoy
Making only the most of a given today, both disappear and gone forever
Backwards and backtracking one can not do with either love or life
Each day that is wasted in a life has become the past
Much like a love that has been wasted on hate
Living is only done is the presence of today
Planning for the future, wanting and dreams of how it will be
Futures plans that never arrive the blend into the reality of just today
Making mistakes in love and sometimes in life
Learning from each and only able to go gone but wiser
Choosing to be embittered by the love or the life one must decide
Regrets that keep the gift of today for truly being cherished
Love should be breath like the air in our lungs that keeps us alive
Inhaled are the precious seconds before needing to breathe again.
If we do not breathe again, then this life starts to end.
Lives without love already rapidly extinguishing
Without love an existence robbed of joy and happiness
Each person life is a story needing to be told
Each experience of loving a legacy of life

Lying Love

Lying love's speaking though the many lost years
Lying love because of all the hidden fears
Loving others because of what can really be expressed
Finding in the end that there are many of life's regrets

Lying love can become expressed because of others needs
Insisting that there is still fire and passion that only we must feed
Needing other lovers and being honest is what we find
Expressing the truth in everything and in them to be kind

Raising the kids or just paying the bills
Continuing the journey that never seems to heal
Looking for acceptance that embraces the heart
Wandering feelings inside the soul do now start

Wanting our lives to fit nicely into the box
Being that mother and wife instead of some sexy fox
Lying love being the person who is near and yet so far
Wishing you were together and wishing on that nighttime stars

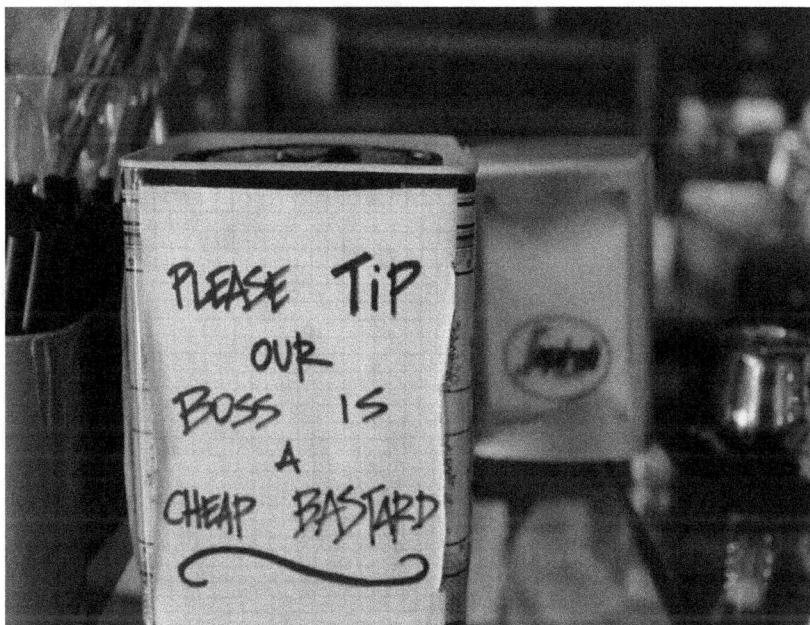

Jerry D. Hayes "Pablito"

Lives in Myrtle Beach, South Carolina- The Father of four children. Tara, Melissa, Jeremy and Jordan Hayes.

Inspired by Pablo Neruda's universal appeal to the beauty of a woman.

JerryDHayes.com

www.ingramcontent.com/pod-product-compliance
Lightning Source LLC
Chambersburg PA
CBHW071838020426
42331CB00007B/1773